W9-CGN-348

# HERE'S
# LIFE!

# HERE'S LIFE!

## TRUE STORIES FROM THE INNER CITY

# TED GANDY

All scripture quotations, unless otherwise indicated, are taken from the Holy Bible: New International Version®. NIV®. Copyright © 1973, 1978, 1984 by International Bible Society. Used by permission of Zondervan Bible Publishers. All rights reserved.

*The names in Here's Life Inner City stories are often changed to protect the privacy of those we help. Also, stories are told in a real time format.

All rights reserved. No part of this book may be reproduced in any form without the written permission of Here's Life Inner City, except brief quotations used in connection with reviews in magazines or newspapers.

ISBN 0-9765594-1-2

Cover and text art by Hampton Creative, Tulsa, OK

© 2005 Campus Crusade for Christ International

Printed in the United States of America.

Here's Life Inner City
142 West 36th Street
New York, NY 10018
Website: www.hlic.org

# DEDICATION

This book is dedicated to the 170 faithful and persevering staff of Here's Life Inner City, who are building a strong legacy for Christ in America's inner cities. Special mention also goes to Jamie Ray, Meredith Gandy, Doug Brendel, and Shelly Roark, without whose assistance this book would not have come to completion.

# TABLE OF CONTENTS

# INTRODUCTION

## LIFE WITH REAL PEOPLE

*You wouldn't have liked James very much if you had met him a few years ago.*

*He was addicted to drugs, a convicted robber, and fresh out of prison. The angry man was always tense and aggressive.*

*And he was very unhappy about attending a substance abuse program. But James had no choice — it was a condition of his prison release. The rehab program was near a large warehouse where James and other participants hung out during session breaks. That's where James met Faye, the Here's Life Inner City warehouse coordinator in Los Angeles.*

*She was so nice ... James couldn't understand it. What did she want?*

*But soon Faye broke through James' tough exterior and learned about his struggles to stay clean. She also heard about his family — Delia and five kids. Finances were tight with such a large family ... and they were struggling to survive.*

*Faye offered the family food from the warehouse. James was grateful, but also confused. Again, what did she want? What was on her mind?*

*He soon found out. Faye shared the message of Christ's
hope and love with James.*

*The next week, he showed up at her church. It wasn't
long before James opened his heart to the Lord. Then Delia
came to church. She said, "I wanted to come because I'm
seeing such a change in James." The kids also came, and
one by one, they all received Christ.*

*Delia told Faye recently, "If you hadn't been at the
warehouse, offering friendship and food, I don't know where
we'd be now. We'd probably still be going down the wrong
road. You just don't know what a difference all this has
made!" The family continues to grow in faith together. Now
James works for a construction contractor and builder from
church and wants nothing to do with drugs or trouble from
his old life. He's a changed man with a sweet disposition —
and a gentleness and peace that come from God. You'd like
him!*

# DEAR COMPASSIONATE FRIEND,

In the pages of this book, you will meet fascinating people ... you will hear unbelievable stories ... and you will witness amazing real life transformations. Just like James.

As incredible as the accounts you are about to read may seem, they are not fictional, because this book is about *real life* in the poverty-stricken areas of urban America. According to the Census Bureau, 35.9 million Americans live below the poverty line. Many are hungry, cold, and homeless. They live from moment to moment, struggling for survival.

The good news is that this book is also about *real help*. My name is Ted Gandy; I'm the national director of Here's Life Inner City, the compassionate urban ministry of Campus Crusade for Christ. For more than 20 years, we've ministered to America's urban poor by helping neighborhood missions and inner-city churches.

We empower local ministries to reach out to the hurting in their communities with food, clothing, programs for children, employment assistance, and so much more. You'll learn about these special partnerships and programs, too, in the following pages.

It is through this network of compassionate care that lives are impacted ... and changed for eternity. To desperate men, women, and children wondering where the next meal will come from or how they will stay warm for the night, our help — fueled by the giving and prayers of friends across

America — is tangible proof of God's love. I have seen over and over again how God can use a box of groceries or a new pair of shoes to open hearts.

Our mission, our mandate, is to put hands and feet to Jesus Christ's love — "Religion that God our Father accepts as pure and faultless is this: to look after orphans and widows in their distress and to keep oneself from being polluted by the world" (James 1:27).

In the following chapters, you will see this Scripture put to action and its impact on lives.

Because, most of all, this book is about *real people*. It is about the frightened child abandoned by her mother. It is about the grandmother wondering how she will feed and clothe her family. It is about the homeless man who lost it all because of drug and alcohol addiction.

The story of Here's Life Inner City is the story of one person at a time, one heart at a time, touched by the love and compassion of God's people. Friends like you who pray and support our outreaches are part of the story, too.

So read and enjoy the following stories of *real* life in God's hands. I promise you will like every person you meet!

God's best,

*Ted Gandy*

TED GANDY
HLIC National Director

## *Chapter 1*

# CARDBOARD BOXES AND OPEN DOORS

*"For he satisfies
the thirsty
and fills the hungry
with good things."*

PSALM 107:9

Bam, bam, bam!

The banging on the door startled Alice. But she didn't have the will or the energy to answer it. She just sat like she had been for the past half hour, staring at the battered old refrigerator — willing something ... *anything*, to be in it.

She had to think. The kids would come running into the small kitchen soon with growling stomachs. Five-year-old Justin was a bottomless pit anyway. Lisette and Lynette, ages 7 and 9, knew times were tough, but they couldn't understand hunger.

What was she going to do about supper? What could she do? Nothing....

Bam, bam, bam!

Great. Were bill collectors going door-to-door now? Alice really didn't care who was there. Whoever it was wasn't about to solve her problem ... maybe they would just go away.

A familiar wave of desperation and fear was starting to spread through her body. What a mess she had made of her life ... and she wasn't even 30 yet! Alice dropped her face down into her hands. Augh! Those hands — gnarled and deformed. She hated them! They had failed her and caused her children to go hungry on more than one occasion. With severely handicapped hands, Alice couldn't easily find a job. So, she was living on public assistance ... if you called that living.

It wasn't so long ago that she had decided she wasn't living anyway ... why not make it official? But she even managed to mess that up.

Bam, bam, bam!

Again? Whoever was there wasn't giving up. She forced herself to get up and walk to the door. Alice rolled her eyes when she looked through the peephole and saw who was waiting outside her door.

*Those* people! Neighbors Allen and Maria stood there grinning ... they *would not leave her alone*. They kept inviting her to church. She had no use for church or its people and precious little time to worry about anything but surviving with three young kids in Queens, New York!

Now, today of all days.... Well, she was prepared to give them a piece of her mind as she swung open the door. But what she wasn't prepared for was what was on the other side of that door — *a cardboard box that would change her life*.

The Box of Love contains all the trappings of a complete holiday meal for an entire family of six, actually enough food for several days by inner-city standards.

Allen shoved the big box toward her as Maria sang out, "Happy Thanksgiving!"

Alice stood speechless. That's right, Thanksgiving was tomorrow. She was too worried about finding something to feed her kids day-by-day to remember a holiday for rich people.

"This is a gift from our church," Maria continued.

Alice's eyes widened as they told her about the Box of Love filled with a turkey, vegetables, fruit, dessert, and more.

It was enough food to feed her family for several days!

Relief and gratitude spilled out of Alice in a rush of tears. The kids came running out to see what was wrong. Seeing the food, they started whooping and hollering. What a feast!

Alice smiled and thanked Allen and Maria over and over again. She was overwhelmed. These people — her neighbors and others she had never even met — were feeding her babies. She didn't know why, but she was going to find out.

The next Sunday, Alice, Justin, Lisette, and Lynette went to church dressed in their best. That very day, Alice asked Christ into her life. It wasn't long before all three children did, too.

The family started attending church each week, and the kids got involved in the children's program. Alice steadily grew in her faith and now feels like she is part of a family with people who care about her.

And she knows God cares about her, too. Not because the preacher says so ... not just because the Bible says so. But because He sent someone to knock on her door when she was in need.

Sometimes a simple cardboard box of food says it all. It is Christ's love revealed in a practical, tangible way for desperate people like Alice. *Here's Life Inner City has had the privilege of partnering with inner-city churches and missions to give out nearly 350,000 of these Boxes of Love since 1987.*

Each year, Here's Life provides at least 25,000 Boxes of Love for our partner ministries to distribute in 16 cities. An additional 5,000 modified Boxes of Love are distributed after the holidays, as well.

And in that time, we have seen over and over again how one simple box of groceries can transform an entire family.

## DOES ANYONE CARE?

Janice was in her late 30s and had already hit bottom. Her husband was so consumed with drugs that he abandoned her and their four children (ages 7 to 15). On top of that, Janice lost her job and was forced to share a single, small apartment with another family. It was cramped, awkward, and uncomfortable.

She knew her children were hurting. But what could she do? She was hurting, too. And no one cared ... no one, except maybe for Karen.

A former co-worker, Karen prayed for Janice and even helped her financially. When she showed up at Janice's apartment with the Box of Love just before Thanksgiving, Janice broke down and wept. Someone did care! Of course her friend cared, but so did the *complete strangers* who provided this box of food. She couldn't believe that anyone would make the effort for her and her children.

Karen and Janice opened the Box of Love together, and Karen talked with Janice about how much God loved her. They went through the enclosed Scripture materials and Janice asked Jesus to come into her life. By the end of the day, all four children had also received Christ!

That Sunday, the whole family went to church. It was a new beginning.

Now the children are very active in Sunday school and other church activities. Janice's new faith helped pull her out of deep depression. She got another job. And through a housing rehab program of the church, she and her children moved out of the crowded apartment and into a house (with the help of a few strong backs from church). Janice also joined a Bible study cell group that sometimes even meets in *her* house.

The story gets even better....

Janice began sharing the Gospel with her brother, but he always resisted. Then he was diagnosed with cancer and hospitalized for treatment. As his condition deteriorated, Janice's brother cried out from his bed: "God, if you are real and what Janice and her friends say is true, I will serve you.... Let me live."

The specific contents of each box vary according to the tastes of the individual community:

- A 12-lb. turkey (with stuffing) or a ham
- Vegetables
- Potatoes
- Juice
- Yams
- Apple or cranberry sauce
- Bread
- Fruit
- Dessert
- Scriptures and children's literature

He recovered — and committed his life to Christ. Subsequent medical tests showed no trace of cancer in his body!

Janice gives God the glory: "Can you believe it? What a snowball effect! First my family, and now my brother. And it all started with a box."

A single box ... *a single act of compassion can change a life and transform an entire family*. It seems incredible. But when you consider God's love for the poor and down-and-out, it's not really surprising.

"He upholds the cause of the oppressed and gives food to the hungry. The Lord sets prisoners free, the Lord gives sight to the blind, the Lord lifts up those who are bowed down, the Lord loves the righteous. The Lord watches over the alien and sustains the fatherless and the widow ..." (Psalm 146:7-9).

To God, *love* is *action*. We're all on the receiving end of that — "Greater love has no one than this, that he lay down his life for his friends" (John 15:13).

There is no better way to honor Christ's sacrifice of love — and point the way to Him — than by putting that same love and compassion into action.

Here are a few more testimony treasures from "the Box":

▓ Pastor Thiem Baccam's church in Minneapolis draws a diverse group of people from the inner city, including many young people (Laotian, Hmong, Cambodian, Filipino, African-American). The target of their Box of Love outreach was the families of these young people. One of these youth, a high school senior named Lee, was a new believer. He wanted his mother to understand the Gospel of Christ. Their background was animist combined with ancestor worship. Lee's mother was paralyzed, confined to a wheel chair for many years. Lee's father had left the family, leaving Lee, Lee's younger sister, and their handicapped mother. Finances were very tight.

When Pastor Baccam arrived at the home with a Box of Love, Lee's mom was happy to receive the wonderful gift of food. As Pastor Baccam shared about the love and forgiveness of Christ, Lee's mother joyfully opened her heart to Him, and immediately she asked if she could come to church. But there was a problem. The church is not wheel chair accessible. The pastor prayed with her that there would be a way she could come to the church. In the meantime, he and others in the church began to visit her at home. About three weeks after the Box of Love delivery, Lee came running up to the pastor. "Thank you, thank you! For the first time in many years, my mom is able to stand up on her own!" She is not yet able to walk, but they are praying that that, too, will happen.

While delivering Boxes of Love in Brooklyn, Debbe, who is the director of the Salt & Sea Mission (an HLIC partner ministry), found a young Hispanic boy digging through garbage cans. It was a daily routine for 10-year-old Martin in the run-down, crime-infested neighborhood. Rain, snow, or shine, he scavenged for bottles to redeem the five-cent

deposit. The money helped provide food for his mom and
baby sister.

When Debbe walked up to him and offered him
a box of food, Martin was astounded. Because the
box was too big for him to carry, she gave him a ride
to his apartment. There, relatives kept pouring out
of crowded rooms in the small apartment. So Debbe
left *two boxes* to feed them all. She told them that
the food was from Jesus and invited them to the
Mission's Thanksgiving service. Martin, his cousin,
and grandparents attended, and they all received
Christ as their Savior!

Mike and Lynn are part of an inner-city church in
Jacksonville, Florida. A few days before Thanksgiving, they
delivered a Box of Love to a family living in a drug-ridden,
violent housing project. Some neighbors had requested the
box for them, knowing Robert had been out of work for a
long time with back troubles. His wife, Isabel, worked hard as
a waitress trying to provide for the family, which included
four girls — 11-year-old twins, a 6-year-old, and a 3-year-old.
Their ailing grandmother also lived with them.

When the volunteers arrived, Isabel was at
work. Robert let them in, but was withdrawn and
distant. The girls, on the other hand, were
overjoyed by a surprise visit from caring strangers.

Mike and Lynn couldn't help but notice the cockroaches and other insects ... the dirty dishes piled in the sink ... the girls running barefoot even though it was already a cold late-November day. *Do they even own shoes?* Lynn wondered silently.

As the visitors talked with the children, the grandmother, Lorraine, warmed to them. Lynn talked about Christ's love. And before they left, Lorraine had asked Jesus into her life! After that, Mike and Lynn prayed for the family and brought new shoes for the girls. The Box of Love visit had made an impact even on the depressed father of the family. "These people acted like they really cared about us," he had told his wife.

It was more of a rescue operation than Mike and Lynn even realized. As they learned, Isabel was almost ready to give up on the marriage. Robert was convinced he would never work again. But Mike challenged Robert to trust God for his future. Lynn inspired Isabel to hang on. The family began attending church. Soon, both parents and all four children had committed their lives to Christ.

The girls got involved in one of our youth development centers. Robert landed a good job in a brake repair shop — beginning as a mechanic, and then managing the whole shop! They have their share of setbacks and hurdles, but the Lord continues to move them forward as a family in their relationship with Him.

These are only a very few of the thousands of positive transformations God has wrought in the lives of inner-city individuals and families across America through Boxes of Love.

These simple cardboard boxes do so much more than hold food ... they open doors!

*Chapter 2*

# SAME
# PLACE ...
# ANY TIME

*"Be patient, then, brothers, until the Lord's coming. See how the farmer waits for the land to yield its valuable crop and how patient he is for the autumn and spring rains. You too, be patient ..."*

JAMES 5:7-8

The fire took almost no time at all to destroy everything they had.

On a small fixed income, Grandmother Hattie was already struggling to make ends meet for herself and her three grandchildren — 9-year-old Makenzie, 11-year-old Chloe, and 13-year-old Cedric. Now her apartment was gone, with everything in it.

The only place they could find to stay was in a building with no heat ... in the dead of a Chicago-area winter — with average temperatures of _26 degrees_!

Desperate, cold, and with no resources to keep her little ones warm, Hattie heard about a place where she could get blankets, warm hats, and gloves — Restoration Ministries, a partner with the Here's Life team in Chicago.

> According to the Census Bureau, 35.9 million Americans live below the poverty line. Almost 20% of children — nearly one out of every five — live in an impoverished family. Many live on the streets or in abandoned buildings.

At Restoration, not only did the family receive winter survival gear in the form of our Homeless Care Kit, but they also heard the Gospel. And the kids _immediately_ put their faith in Christ!

They became regulars at the Restoration after-school program as well, which features computers for homework, nutritious meals, and a Bible club.

For this family, receiving the critical winter resources found in our Homeless Care Kits sparked an immediate transformation. It didn't take them long to connect the practical, tangible act of compassion with God's love. A single act of kindness ignited change that put their world right.

But it doesn't always happen so quickly.

For many of the desperate people in our nation's inner cities, particularly the homeless, a single act doesn't cut it. A moment of help can be too easily forgotten in the day-after-day, minute-by-minute fight for survival.

It's only through persevering kindness that they can begin to see the light of hope.

Take, John, for example. He was a tough case....

## WORTH THE WAIT

John had already lived more than a half a century — most of it on the streets of Brooklyn — when he met Iris and her team of volunteers passing out Homeless Care Kits.

John lived in a "squatter's house," a little room he had built himself out of cardboard boxes. Every day, he collected bottles from streets and alleyways. He could get five cents a piece for them at the local grocery store. That's what John lived on ... at least that's what he used to feed his drug and alcohol habits.

One cold winter day, Iris and others from their church's Mission of Mercy outreach were giving hot soup and coffee to people living on the streets when they came upon John. He was more than happy to accept the blanket, gloves, and hat they offered him from the Homeless Care Kit.

But that was as far as he would let them go. He *did not* want to hear about anything spiritual! He *did not* want them telling him how to change his life!

So they kept quiet and put their ministry into action. They visited John, brought him food and blankets, and prayed for him. Weeks went by ... months went by ... years went by. No visible change. Still, they visited John, they brought him food and blankets, and prayed for him.

This group of determined volunteers cared for John for *five years*!

Then, finally, came the long-awaited breakthrough....

One Thanksgiving, the Mission of Mercy group cooked food from Boxes of Love at their church to serve the homeless. As Iris came out of the kitchen with the first course of the meal, she was shocked to see John. The lure of a Thanksgiving feast had actually gotten him inside a church!

During the dinner, men from a local Christian drug and alcohol rehabilitation center shared personal testimonies and challenged the people to start life over through faith in Christ.

Early the next morning, John appeared at the door of the rehabilitation center. He heard the Word of God and gave his life to Christ. John spent a year at the center, turning away from drugs and alcohol and growing in his faith.

The day he graduated from the program, Iris and her husband were in the audience as his "family." John told the audience it was the active love and persistence of Iris and the others that made the difference for him.

Today, John is the superintendent of a large apartment building in Brooklyn. He has his own apartment and owns a car. The once-angry, defensive drug addict has been transformed into a caring, loving man because acts of kindness became something he could count on. It was worth the wait!

## ARMS OF COMPASSION ALWAYS OPEN

Tommy's story is another example of a life in slow metamorphosis.

He never was a "typical" street person. Tommy had it all at age 40. A decorated Vietnam veteran, he had a master's degree, taught at a large university, and dabbled in the insurance business. Tommy was wealthy and never dreamed that he would one day live on the streets. But his life took a dramatic downhill turn....

After a divorce, Tommy married Terry, even though he knew her only a month. Then he discovered she was addicted to heroin. Not long after their wedding, Terry discovered she was HIV-positive and dropped into deep depression. Terry soon found "happiness" again in cocaine.

Tommy kept buying more cocaine to keep his wife happy. Pretty soon, he began to use, too. The habit took all his financial resources and left them destitute. Tommy decided that he and Terry were pulling each other down. Despairing, he walked out.

He found his way to Salt & Sea Mission, a partner ministry on Coney Island, New York, for food. But he wanted nothing to do with God. Sometimes he had a place to live ... other times not. When the weather turned cold, Tommy turned to the mission for a Homeless Care Kit. Still, he didn't want any more involvement.

Months went by. Because of his drug habit, Tommy couldn't hold down a regular job. He became a courier for a local drug dealer. Then winter winds blew in the cold, and again Tommy went to Salt & Sea. Again, they gave him winter survival gear from a Care Kit. This time, however, Tommy stayed around a bit longer and listened to the message. Maybe he would turn his life over to God. But soon the lure of drugs was too strong.

This cycle went on for several *years*. Whenever Tommy was in need, he went to the same place ... Salt & Sea. He always knew where to find them. And they always helped him.

Eventually, Tommy found the real help he needed. After years of seeing the fruits of God's love in action, Tommy committed his life fully to God. He told the workers at Salt & Sea that God's consistency and faithfulness was demonstrated to him through the Homeless Care Kits.

He realized that, no matter what he had done, God was still reaching out to him.

> Winter conditions that merely inconvenience many can be deadly for the homeless. This winter, God will use friends like you to provide 8,300 Homeless Care Kits for people in need.

Today, Tommy is drug-free, holds a full-time job with a building contractor, and volunteers three nights a week at the Salt & Sea Mission. Tommy still attends several Bible studies there.

For Tommy, John, and many other needy people in our inner cities, change does not happen — cannot happen — overnight. Because for the homeless, a single moment doesn't transform their world. It takes time. It takes workers who are there day after day after day, and year after year after year ... sharing God's hope and love in practical ways. Often it is not a single event, but persistence and determination in Christ's name that changes someone's world.

We share this commitment with generous supporters, volunteers, and workers in churches and missions across America. They never give up on the homeless, the lost, and the needy because God never gives up. He is always waiting ... same place, any time.

A Homeless Care Kit includes:

- Warm gloves and a snug woolen stocking cap ...
- A scarf to protect against the biting winds ...
- Socks to warm numb feet ...
- A thick blanket wrap to keep out the icy night ...
- Basics like a toothbrush, soap, and even underwear in some cases ...
- Most importantly, a brand-new New Testament.

"Here I am! I stand at the door and knock. If anyone hears my voice and opens the door, I will come in and eat with him, and he with me" (Revelation 3:20).

# TESTIMONY SPOTLIGHT

## PRODIGAL SON RETURNS HOME

Denver, Colorado, is a beautiful place to live — except in the cold months, if you live under a bridge.

That's where Danny found himself one winter.

He had been raised in a Christian home, but turned away from his faith. After serving in Vietnam, Danny began using alcohol and drugs to escape the haunting memories of war. He couldn't hold a job, and his family cut him off.

So there he was — alone, hungry, cold, and huddled under a bridge.

He tried to sleep with one eye open to safeguard his bag of meager belongings from thieves. Still, one morning he woke up and found that all his worldly possessions were gone.

Danny made his way to Christ's Body Ministries, a partner ministry with Here's Life Inner City in Denver, where he heard they had food and, even more importantly, winter gear: blankets, hats, and gloves. One of the other guys he knew from under the bridge had frozen to death. Danny didn't want that to happen to him.

At Christ's Body Ministries, Danny found hot coffee, friendly people, and a warm blanket. He also found someone he had lost along the way — God. He recommitted his life to Christ.

Danny continued living under the bridge, wrapped up in his blanket at night. But during the day, he participated in the mission's "one step" program, Alcoholics Christian Fellowship. There, he learned to trust Christ to overcome his addiction to alcohol and drugs.

Once Danny's life was stabilized, he started their employment program, gaining actual work experience at several small businesses the ministry runs (house painting, carting, lawn and garden care, building maintenance).

Danny eventually got a job as an auto mechanic, and he is now self-supporting. He continues to grow strong in his faith and has been reconciled with members of his family.

Danny has come home.

*Chapter 3*

# NO

# FAIRY TALES

# HERE

"*To comfort all who mourn, and provide for those who grieve in Zion — to bestow on them a crown of beauty instead of ashes, the oil of gladness instead of mourning, and a garment of praise instead of a spirit of despair. They will be called oaks of righteousness, a planting of the Lord for the display of his splendor.*"

ISAIAH 61:2-3

When the monthly check ran out by the last week of January, Jenny and her mother moved into a shelter in downtown Los Angeles.

The shelter was near one of our S.A.Y. Yes! Centers for Youth Development, run by a local church. On Tuesday, 6-year-old Jenny wandered in very quietly, sucking her thumb for security. She heard Bible stories and helped make rice crispy treats for dessert after dinner.

By Wednesday, she started opening up. She participated in fun new exercises, played games, ate, and learned some more about Jesus. Then came Thursday, Jenny's 7th birthday!

Through neighborhood churches, our S.A.Y. Yes! Centers for Youth Development (S.A.Y. stands for *Save America's Youth*) provide a haven during the hours of 3 to 8 p.m. when inner-city kids are most at risk.

www.sayyescenters.org

When she arrived at the Center, Jenny's eyes grew wide and her mouth dropped open at the big poster with "Happy Birthday, Jenny!" in bright colors and fancy writing. There was even a neatly wrapped present for her. Jenny couldn't believe it! And after dinner, they turned out all the lights but the glowing candles on her birthday cake. Jenny grinned from ear to ear as her new friends sang to her. It was a birthday like none other ... her first birthday party ever!

I happened to be visiting the Center that day and was thrilled to participate in the celebration. Jenny's face was something to see. I didn't think anything could ruin that day for her.

But later that night, Krista, a volunteer from the Center, took Jenny back to the shelter. Jenny's mother was nowhere to be found. The little girl's heart sank as she realized the terrible truth: her mom wasn't coming back. One of the best days of her life quickly hit rock bottom.

The first-of-the-month check had arrived that day, and Jenny's mom took off ... abandoning her little one on her birthday.

As they waited for a social worker to arrive from Child Protective Services, Jenny tried to hold back the stinging tears. She talked to Krista about the past week and how much fun she had at the Center. The frightened 7-year-old clung to her birthday gift and asked Krista if they could pray. Jenny closed her eyes, squeezed Krista's hand and prayed ... for her mother. Then she was taken away into the custody of the state of California.

Real life stories don't always have happy endings.

And sometimes, workers at our S.A.Y. Yes! Centers never know what will happen when a child walks out the door. They have no idea what the end result will be. Still, they keep working to impact lives ... one small chapter at a time.

Here's Life is privileged to partner with local churches and communities to provide resources, training, and curriculum for after-school S.A.Y. Yes! Centers (*S.A.Y.* stands for *Save America's Youth*) in over 100 inner-city neighborhoods. They focus on encouraging at-risk youngsters, helping them do well in school through tutoring and mentoring and introducing them to Christ.

The Centers get them off the streets and into a loving, productive atmosphere ... something many of these needy children will not find at home. Typically, kids at the Centers have a snack, work on computers, play games, take field trips, get help with homework, do Bible studies, and eat dinner before they go home! Staff members love and bond with these youth, writing messages of God's love on their hearts.

And God takes it from there....

"Jenny's story represents the many children who move in and out of our Center. Some stay longer than others. Some, like Jenny, only for a week. But of all weeks, God allowed us to share her life during her birthday week. Her eyes and heart saw and felt something that was different. Something special. And those special people talked about Jesus."

# A STRONG FOUNDATION

Felix came to the Agape Center, home of our S.A.Y Yes! Center in the Roseland area of south Chicago, at age 11.

He'd heard from friends that it was a good place to go after school — there were sports like basketball and other games — an improvement over streets and glass-strewn playgrounds. After participating in a Bible study at the Center, he put his faith in Christ. And he began to meet weekly with staff member Marc for discipleship training. In spite of the chaos of his neighborhood, Felix seemed to be well grounded.

Then, when Felix was 13, his mom moved him and his younger brother out of Roseland to a more suburban area. It seemed like a good idea, but it took Felix away from his friends at the Agape Center and from Marc. Sadly, Felix's life took a dark turn.

As a young teen trying to prove himself in a new neighborhood, Felix thought he needed more money than his hardworking single mom could provide. The only way he knew to get money at his age was through drugs ... and the only way to get into that scene was through a gang. He turned away from the truths he had been learning.

For the next five years, Felix lived in hell. He smoked weed, drank alcohol, and got kicked out of three different high schools for gang activity and fighting. He was thrown in and out of jail — and he saw more than one guy just like himself get *killed*.

He knew he needed help. He tried reading the Bible again, but it didn't make the same kind of sense it used to make. It just wasn't clear. Occasionally when times were the darkest, Felix would pray: "God, get me out of this and I'll come back to you." But by the next day, he would jump back into the thick of street life.

> S.A.Y. Yes! Centers establish a safe, stable, affirming environment with culturally relevant activities appealing to children, including games, mentoring, Bible study, tutoring, computer training, and field trips which expose kids to different options in life. Church volunteers serve as leaders, teachers, and mentors.

Still, God wasn't ready to close the book on Felix. He gave him yet another chance ... in the form of a residential military school. Felix, however, didn't make things easy — the night before he was to leave for school, he got into more trouble and ended up in court. He could have been jailed — but the judge released him to get on the bus for military school.

Away from the influence of his gang and without drugs or alcohol, Felix's head began to clear. He was drawn to his

Bible and began to read again. This time it made more sense to him.

God brought to his mind the truths he had learned at the Agape Center. He began to pray and revive his faith. But there would be another twist to the story ... one that threatened to send Felix back into the world of gangs.

While Felix was away, his cousin was killed in a gang-related incident. As he stood looking at the coffin during the funeral, a battle raged within Felix. He owed it to his cousin to make the rival gang pay! He *had* to retaliate. Yet he knew that this was a turning point in his life. He had been doing well for several months — if he gave in to revenge, he would lose it all forever. He would be trapped in his old lifestyle. And he knew God would not be honored.

Finally, Felix made his decision. He got on the bus and went back to school. In six months, he earned his GED and proudly walked across the stage to receive his diploma.

The young man eventually returned to Chicago. Today, he is married with two children and works for the U.S. Postal Service.

As Felix's life began to be grounded again in the Lord, he and Marc reconnected. Eventually, Marc asked if Felix would help him lead a Practical Christian Living group for some young men from the neighborhood ... the place where that first seed of the Gospel had been planted in Felix.

Felix brings a unique perspective to the group, warning about wrong choices. "I know God brought me out to be a witness," he says.

> The children of S.A.Y. Yes! are growing up with this program. Today, 25% are in junior or senior high school. So we're enhancing our training and equipping of S.A.Y. Yes! Centers to engage teens effectively. We're focusing especially on sexual purity, independence from welfare (via education and entrepreneurial skills), character development, and spiritual accountability.

At the Agape Center and elsewhere, Felix shares the testimony of God's grace in his life. Last year he even preached a sermon! His story has come full circle.

With God as the author, real life *can* have happy endings.

# SCRIPTURE IN ACTION

## GOD'S WORD CHANGES STORY'S END!

Fourteen-year-old Tanya lives in the Fairfax area of Bakersfield, California ... a neighborhood that seems like the end of the earth. There is no entertainment, not even a single restaurant — and absolutely nothing for kids to do. The city buses don't even go to Fairfax. The only things this area has plenty of are poverty, drug traffic, and physical abuse.

From all accounts, the story of Tanya's life looked like it was heading for a typical ending full of tragedy and despair.

But when a small mission church in the area opened a S.A.Y. Yes! Center, Tanya went to check it out.

Church was the last place anyone expected to see Tanya ... a "trash-talking troublemaker." But the Center's workers looked past her rough exterior and offered compassion and care. Christ's love slowly took root in Tanya's heart and began to blossom.

She started hanging around for Wednesday night church activities. Then she began showing up on Sunday mornings, too. Tanya turned from troublemaker to peacemaker. Even the foul words were soon weeded out of Tanya's language.

The seed of the Gospel planted in Tanya yielded a gentle young lady — quite a different ending to her story!

Then it was Tanya's turn to bring a new ending to someone else's life story.

Her father, Arthur, was in jail when Tanya started going to the S.A.Y. Yes! Center. He had been a major ringleader of trouble in the neighborhood. But when he got out of jail, Arthur was amazed at the change in his daughter.

She began bringing him to the church, and, after three visits, he, too, received Christ. Today, whenever Arthur talks about the changes in his life, tears come to his eyes. He has a job, his own foul language has changed, and he has established a daily accountability time with the pastor to help him keep going in the right direction. He's hungry to know God!

God used Here's Life Inner City supporters to change these lives through the S.A.Y. Yes! program. Now that's a happy ending!

*Chapter 4*

# EVERYTHING'S

# UNDER

# CONTROL ...

# REALLY

*"Your eyes saw my unformed body.*
*All the days ordained for me*
*were written in your book*
*before one of them came to be.*
*How precious to me are your thoughts, O God!*
*How vast is the sum of them!"*

PSALM 139:16-17

Vivian had it all — a husband she loved and a house blessed with the pitter-patter of little feet (they had three children and another on the way).

But then it all fell apart.

At a seven-month pre-natal checkup, Vivian's doctor shattered her world with these words: "You have tested positive for HIV."

Vivian was speechless. It was the last thing on earth she expected to hear. She had never been a drug user and had always been faithful to her husband. The test couldn't be right, could it?

The doctor strongly recommended that the rest of her family get tested. All the children (including the new baby, eventually) tested negative. But Vivian's husband turned out HIV-positive. She was devastated to discover that he had been living a secret life of adultery for years. Now the deadly consequences of his sinful lifestyle had spread to Vivian.

To make matters worse, Vivian's husband became so enraged about his diagnosis — and that his secret was out — that he turned violent. He began abusing Vivian.

Vivian was in a state of shock. This was a bad dream — her whole world was spinning out of control, her children's future in jeopardy — and now, domestic violence. But she didn't tell anyone ... not her friends ... not her family. She couldn't — she was too ashamed and depressed.

As her husband's violence increased, Vivian knew she had to get herself and her children out of harm's way. She fled to a shelter for people with HIV, but her depression increased. She began to think about killing herself — how could she face such a painful future? But then what would happen to her children? What would happen to them anyway? She had no idea how she was going to feed, clothe, and care for four children by herself.

Though she had no spiritual background, Vivian began to cry out to God. Her circumstances were too heavy to carry alone. Gradually, she began to move towards Him. And God began gently, lovingly revealing Himself to her.

> From Here's Life Inner City warehouses, we initiate our Homeless Care Kit, Box of Love, and Easter Bag evangelistic outreaches — plus training for partners in ministry for evangelism, follow-up, and discipleship.

The Drew University Center for Health Services Research AIDS program is right around the corner from our Here's Life Inner City warehouse in Los Angeles. One day, the director of the program saw food being delivered and unloaded at the warehouse. He came over and talked with Faye, our warehouse manager. He told her about the many struggling AIDS patients who came to his program — most couldn't work because they were so debilitated. And the program's resources didn't meet all the needs of their families. Could his clients receive food from the warehouse? he asked.

Faye explained that food was not distributed at the warehouse, but through local churches. However, Faye said, she would be happy to connect their clients with partner churches so they could receive food through them. If a client was physically unable to go to the church to receive food, church workers would take it to them.

When Vivian, who was one of the program clients, learned of the new opportunity, she knew this God she was just getting to know was providing for her and her children.

As Vivian grew in faith and in strength, she began to volunteer at the clinic where she herself had been a resident. She did so well that the clinic hired her to work in their office. Today, she shares with the many patients who come in and out of the clinic doors how God is becoming real in her life. And Vivian has regular contact with Faye, who is encouraging her in her walk with the Lord.

Of course, Vivian is still uncertain about her future, but she is certain about one thing — God has it all under control. She has seen that God is faithful, and she knows He will take care of her children.

## GOD'S RESOURCES

Five different Here's Life Inner City warehouses in major cities across the U.S. serve as God's hands of compassion and provision to the needy.

There are many men, women, and children like Vivian whose lives have spun out of control. Whether because of divorce, drug or alcohol addiction, or a lost job, they are looking up from the bottom.

The Census Bureau reports that 35.9 million Americans lived in poverty in 2003. According to the U.S. Agriculture Department for the same year, nearly 3.8 million families were hungry — so poor that someone in the home skipped meals because the family could not afford them.

> Five regional warehouses — in New York, Los Angeles, Chicago, Minneapolis, and Bakersfield — offer 28,600 total square feet of assistance.

Those who live in such desperation must wonder if anyone cares about them ... about their children. It is certainly hard to hear and accept a message of love in your heart while your stomach is growling. Does God care? Does He have a plan? Or are we on our own?

That's where our warehouse ministry comes in.

Through our five regional warehouses — in New York, Los Angeles, Chicago, Minneapolis, and Bakersfield — we enable more than 400 churches and ministries to connect personally, face-to-face, heart-to-heart, with needy people of the inner city.

> Food for more than 450,000 people each month is distributed through partnering neighborhood ministries.

These workers give practical, tangible proof of God's message: "Yes, I do care about you. I care about your needs and your family. I have a plan to meet those needs and a plan for your life. I love you."

In the past year, our warehouses reached 7,000 with Homeless Care Kits, 30,000 families with Boxes of Love, 36,500 children with Easter Bags, 2,330 with school "PowerPack" backpacks (containing school supplies and a children's Bible), 2,600 with back-to-school shoes, and thousands upon thousands with urgently needed food.

Our warehouses enable partner churches and ministries to serve more than 450,000 meals every month. Since September 2002, our New York City warehouse alone has provided 40,000 pounds of food to the poor each month.

Though food is the primary resource in the warehouse, other items are often donated, including clothing and toys. Sometimes something unusual shows up, but God always has a recipient in mind....

## SPECIAL NEEDS, UNIQUE SOLUTIONS

The day we received several hundred cases of pet food, we wondered what to do with them. But it wasn't long before we got a call from a ministry that works primarily with senior citizens. They had discovered that some seniors were giving their own meager food resources to their pets, which in many cases were their only companions. Consequently, the seniors were becoming malnourished. By any chance, they inquired, did we have any pet food? God had already provided for the need!

Not long ago, Maria, one of our warehouse managers, received a call. Someone had bunk beds to donate ... 14 of them! Together with two dressers that had just been donated, all this furniture took up a lot of space in the warehouse. A few weeks went by, and some of the beds were taken, but five still remained. They were taking up too much space, but Maria felt that God had a family in mind for those beds. So the beds would stay until God was ready.

One Sunday at church, Maria saw a six-month-old baby with cotton in his ears. She looked for Sandra, the baby's mother, to find out why. It was with great difficulty that Sandra admitted the problem. Everyone in the family slept with cotton in his or her ears so cockroaches wouldn't crawl in during the night. They had no beds. *They all slept on the floor*.

Since Sandra's husband abandoned them three years ago, the family had been struggling. He left when Sandra was diagnosed with lupus. He said he couldn't cope with the illness and all the children (there were seven children, plus Sandra's nephew, and the six-month-old baby). Sandra's illness had debilitated her to such an extent that she could no longer work, and she was trying to support the family on her $425-a-month disability check. Her two oldest children worked part-time and pooled resources with their mom. But that didn't leave anything left over for "extras" — like furniture or clothing.

The beds were meant for them! Just when it seemed like nothing was going to go right for this family, God provided them bunk beds and two dressers.

When the furniture arrived at their home, the children danced around as if it were a party. One of the daughters was especially glad for the dressers; she had been storing her clothes in a garbage bag. Every morning as she dressed for school, she had to empty out the bag to find something to wear.

But God wasn't finished! A donation to the warehouse — clothing from the Gap, Old Navy, and Banana Republic —

enabled Maria to supply this struggling family with new clothes ... something they hadn't had in *three years*.

God had thought of everything! He had a plan to give them all they needed ... as He always does —

"Every good and perfect gift is from above, coming down from the Father of the heavenly lights, who does not change like shifting shadows" (James 1:17).

*O Lord, you have searched me*
*and you know me.*
*You know when I sit and when I rise;*
*you perceive my thoughts from afar.*
*You discern my going out and my lying down;*
*you are familiar with all my ways.*
*Before a word is on my tongue*
*you know it completely, O Lord.*
*You hem me in-behind and before;*
*you have laid your hand upon me.*
*Such knowledge is too wonderful for me,*
*too lofty for me to attain.*
*Where can I go from your Spirit?*
*Where can I flee from your presence?*
*If I go up to the heavens, you are there;*
*if I make my bed in the depths, you are there.*
*If I rise on the wings of the dawn,*
*if I settle on the far side of the sea,*
*even there your hand will guide me,*
*your right hand will hold me fast.*
*If I say, "Surely the darkness will hide me*
*and the light become night around me,"*
*even the darkness will not be dark to you;*
*the night will shine like the day,*
*for darkness is as light to you.*
*For you created my inmost being;*
*you knit me together in my mother's womb.*

*I praise you because I am fearfully and wonderfully made;*
*your works are wonderful,*
*I know that full well.*
*My frame was not hidden from you*
*when I was made in the secret place.*
*When I was woven together in the depths of the earth,*
*your eyes saw my unformed body.*
*All the days ordained for me*
*were written in your book*
*before one of them came to be.*
*How precious to me are your thoughts, O God!*
*How vast is the sum of them!*
*Were I to count them,*
*they would outnumber the grains of sand.*
*When I awake,*
*I am still with you.*

PSALM 139:1-18

*Chapter 5*

# THE TANGIBLE
# TOUCH OF
# COMPASSION

*"Suppose a brother or sister is without
clothes and daily food. If one of you says to
him, 'Go, I wish you well; keep warm and
well fed,' but does nothing about his
physical needs, what good is it?"*

JAMES 2:15-16

Carlos is 7 years old and he doesn't like to be touched.

You can talk to him, play with him, even smile at him ... but don't pat him on the head or put your hand on his shoulder. And most important of all, *do not hug him*. Don't you dare!

Carlos has been touched before, and he didn't like it very much.

> PowerPacks are backpacks filled with school supplies distributed through S.A.Y. Yes! Centers, usually at the beginning of the school year. The basic contents include pencils, an eraser, calculator, notebooks, a pen, crayons, a geometry kit, and a student Bible.

For four of the seven years of his short life, Carlos lived in foster care. Some grown-ups he stayed with said they liked him, but then sent him away. Others said they loved him, but they touched him and made him feel bad. He hated them! They didn't love him!

Now he lives with his grandmother. The judge said so.

Grandma says God loves Carlos. But he doesn't believe it. "Nobody loves me!"

Carlos thinks living with his grandmother is OK, except that they don't have any money. That means no backpack for school and no new shoes. How Carlos wants just one pair of shoes for school, and a backpack like all the other kids!

But then, Carlos never gets anything he wants.

One day, Grandma tells Carlos some church people are going to *give* him *new shoes* and a *brand-new backpack* ... with *new stuff* in it!

When she gives him his gifts, Carlos is so excited that he can't stop jumping. The backpack is full of school supplies, and there is a children's Bible inside, too. Grandma tells Carlos that God has provided these things for him because He loves Carlos. Carlos thinks about that.

Then they sit down together and look through Carlos' new book. She reads to him about Jesus' love and kindness. She reads how He loved Carlos enough to *die for him*, and was always with him to care for him.

For the first time, Carlos really *feels* loved. He starts to cry. He isn't sad, but he just can't help it.

With tears streaming down his face, Carlos looks up at his grandmother: "Grandma," he says, "maybe God does love me."

The little 7-year-old's heart is so full of joy that he feels like he will explode if he doesn't touch someone. He wants to hug his grandmother. So he does.

It is a miracle, really.

Transformations like this happen over and over again across America every time we place a PowerPack or new pair of shoes in a needy child's hands for the new school year.

With a simple gesture of practical love, we touch a life.

As friends and partners provide the funds, we send out PowerPacks to 2,330 children through inner-city churches and S.A.Y. Yes! Centers in 12 cities nationwide. And to the children who receive them, these backpacks and shoes are miracles.

## PRACTICAL LOVE

Kesha never dreamed of having anything new for school. She was about to enter the sixth grade in Little Rock, Arkansas, but really hadn't planned on going much anyway.

It was just too embarrassing. Her grandmother couldn't afford to buy her school supplies, and she had to borrow or steal what she needed to get her work done. Besides, school didn't seem to matter much to all the gang members she knew.

Yes, you read that correctly — *gang members*. And no, this pre-teen didn't get involved with a gang from hanging out on the streets or at school ... she *lives* with them.

Kesha — whose mom is always in and out of jail — lives with her grandmother and her two younger brothers. It's actually her grandmother's other children who have made their home a notorious gang hangout.

As she approached sixth grade, Kesha was beginning to see no use for school. But then this bright girl received a miracle — in the form of a simple backpack.

This "PowerPack" backpack, distributed through the S.A.Y. Yes! Center in her neighborhood, was full of brand-new school supplies — and it gave her the confidence to persevere at school despite her difficult home circumstances. Kesha also began to be a regular at the S.A.Y. Yes! Center. There, caring adults helped her with her schoolwork ... and introduced her to the Savior.

"Before PowerPacks, I used to see kids carrying their schoolwork either loose or in whatever kind of carrier they could find, including plastic grocery bags. When the PowerPacks arrive, the children are literally jumping for joy. They run around with happiness and excitement. It is seldom that children in their situation get anything fresh and new."

— Bernice, volunteer leader, S.A.Y. Yes! Center
Abundant Life, Roosevelt, Long Island

She opened her heart to Christ and was baptized in the church that hosts the Center.

Her brothers also began coming to the Center, and their lives have been changed too. "All three children have received

Christ," the Center director says. "They've gone from poor behavior to good behavior. In school, the boys are catching up — and Kesha made the honor roll!"

> Last year, we distributed PowerPacks to 2,330 children through inner-city churches and S.A.Y. Yes! Centers in 12 cities nationwide.

Today, they're developing Christian character. They have hope for the future. They want to be different from the gang members who hang out at their home. The boys want to be policemen when they grow up. And "even though everyone around them lies," the director says, "they won't lie even if telling the truth will get them into trouble. They have learned the principle of honesty at S.A.Y. Yes!"

## POWERPACKS IMPACT ENTIRE FAMILY

Children are not the only ones touched by the practical compassion of a PowerPack.

When volunteers from Broadway Temple in the city of Louisville, Kentucky, knocked on one inner-city door with the backpacks, they helped change the lives of an entire family!

Church volunteers had already visited the home once and invited the three children they knew of to attend their brand-new S.A.Y. Yes! after-school center. But it was when they delivered PowerPacks filled with free gifts for the children that the mom, Helena, opened up. "Backpacks, too? I don't believe it!" she said.

The workers found out that there were actually five children in her family, plus two more who belonged to her boyfriend Steve. Helena said that Steve was the father of her younger children and worked hard to be a father to the others, but battled alcohol. And with so many children, they struggled financially. The backpacks and after-school care would make such a difference!

Right then, Helena opened her heart to Jesus. Her children began to thrive in the S.A.Y. Yes! Center ... but she and Steve still refused to attend church. After members of the church delivered a Box of Love filled with food to the family, Helena and the children showed up at church. They became more and more involved in the church, and gradually Steve came, too. He accepted Christ, and the couple married! They continue to grow spiritually under the practical love and prayers of their church family.

It's our privilege to help friends and partners from across the nation reach out to the needy children and families of America's inner cities ... offering a tangible touch of Christ's compassion — through PowerPacks! God uses them as part of the transformation process in their lives.

*Chapter 6*

# THE

# DOMINO

# EFFECT

*"Those who had been scattered
preached the word wherever they went ...
But the word of God continued
to increase and spread."*

ACTS 8:4, 12:24

This chapter does not end. (Don't get nervous. I'm speaking metaphorically.)

There are lots of new beginnings, but no endings.

For instance, we'll start with Patrick.

He was homeless and hustling drugs when he found Jesus Christ. That moment is when his life really began. Then Patrick met Mark, a Here's Life staff member, and began studying and praying with him. They spent hours and hours together. Patrick even lived with Mark and his family as they discipled him and helped him stay off the streets.

Holistic Hardware is a biblically-based life-skills class on video. It's now used around the country. Developed at a Christian homeless shelter, the "tools" of Holistic Hardware offer the instruction and inspiration needed to develop independent, stable, productive, and self-sufficient lives for those who have been in crisis. There are 10 "tools," including Responsibility, Planning, Work, Love, and Faith.

Patrick's life was so completely transformed that he felt a burning desire to help others like himself. So, Patrick joined the Here's Life Inner City ministry team and began leading our Holistic Hardware courses throughout New York City.

The Holistic Hardware program empowers the homeless and chronically unemployed by focusing on 10 different issues that will get them motivated and equipped for a successful spiritual, personal, and vocational life. Dramatic vignettes and testimonies on video of people who have completed the program reinforce the lessons on subjects like responsibility, planning, discipline, and finances.

Joe was among the students in Patrick's first class.

Joe's earliest memory is of his mother's harsh words: "You are a mental case. You will never amount to anything!" Throughout his life, those words rang in Joe's head.

After school, Joe worked in the computer field. But the echo of his mother's words followed him everywhere. He couldn't hold a job. The only thing he seemed to be able to do was gamble.

After he worked on a job for a while, Joe would quit and take his money to the racetrack. When he won, he felt good — he'd proved his mother wrong. But inevitably he lost. Then he would have to find another job.

Soon Joe's gambling addiction overpowered him. He ran out of money and lost the ability to pick himself up and go to work again. A broken man, he began living on the streets of New York.

A very hungry Joe was drawn to The Lamb's, one of Here's Life Inner City's ministry partners, for food. While there, he learned about the Holistic Hardware class that

Patrick was just beginning. Tired of living on a roller coaster, Joe signed up.

Our course content is based on the Bible, and when Patrick told him that God loved him deeply, Joe at first resisted. But week after week, the message penetrated his soul, and Joe finally asked Christ into his life.

In November, Joe graduated from the course. Now he has a full-time job back in the computer field, and he has become part of the body of believers at The Lamb's where he is growing in his faith.

> Holistic Hardware helps move people in crisis into productive, self-sufficient lives through 10 video sessions and ongoing mentoring from volunteers. At the heart of this program: acquisition of life skills.

This is what Here's Life Inner City is committed to: real life transformation. We do everything in our power to help the down-trodden people of our inner cities rise above their situations. We've designed programs like Holistic Hardware to give people like Patrick and Joe the opportunity to stand on their own two feet, with self-respect and self-confidence.

CareerLink is another valuable tool that has impacted life after life....

## REAL WORLD HELP

Spring had come to the end of the line when she found hope through CareerLink.

Born in Arkansas, Spring was named after a Tanya Tucker country song about a girl born into poverty and hardship whose life turned out well. It proved an accurate prophecy.

Though she dropped out of high school in her junior year, Spring received her diploma through GED studies. She married, had two sons and a daughter, and worked in a craft business. But when her marriage ended in divorce, Spring could not find work that would pay enough for living expenses and childcare. She turned to the state for help.

The State of Arkansas offers 24 months of assistance to help single moms get established in a self-sufficient life. They offer women the choice of programs to help them move out of poverty. Spring chose CareerLink at The Church at Rock Creek.

The CareerLink curriculum, developed by members of our staff — Paul and Shirley, who teach many of the classes — incorporates practical work and social skills training, supported by biblical principles and a clear Gospel message. Topics include résumé preparation, interview preparation and practice, identifying and overcoming barriers to employment, how to market yourself, parenting, and business culture.

Participants receive course materials which include a Holistic Hardware Bible. Every session ends with a Foundation of Hope message by a local pastor, encouraging them to turn to the Lord as they seek to change their lives.

Spring says she walked into CareerLink consumed with discouragement. "But there I felt embraced and hopeful," she says. "I was given skills and tools to move forward in my life. More importantly, I heard over and over again — 'God loves you,' 'He'll never give up on you,' 'He'll always be with you.'"

Spring committed her life to the Lord, and she began attending The Church at Rock Creek. The pastor and people there were supportive and caring — she says it felt like family. Soon her older son, Blake, asked Jesus into his life.

The last session in the course is a job fair where employers interview the women as prospective employees. Just about every woman who completes CareerLink lands a job!

Spring started working at the church ... and now she actually leads the CareerLink program!

"It's awesome," she says, "to stand in front of a group of women and say, 'Two years ago I was where you are. I've learned how to turn my life over to God, and He's been blessing me.'"

Many of these women have heard for years that they are worthless failures. They have been hurt by others and by their own actions, and left with low self-esteem and low expectations for their lives. Many have built walls to protect themselves. But through the love and encouragement at CareerLink, those walls start to come down.

"The women need to know they're not alone in their struggles," Spring says. "I tell them it doesn't matter what's happened in the past. God loves you and He wants you to succeed. You can take today and turn your life around — just make sure God is in the center of all you do."

Spring remembers Vicky, who enrolled in CareerLink last fall. She had a very hard life, no family support, two kids to raise, and no job. Through CareerLink, Vicky gained the skills she needed to get a good job with benefits, and she recently got a promotion. Through the classes, Vicky also placed her faith in Christ.

> Here's Life Inner City also offers WorkNet, a program with self-assessment and career skills which provides a range of training including budgeting, parenting, living God's way, and more.

"I truly love my job," Vicky says, "and I know now that everything has happened for a reason. It just makes you realize that only God knows where you are going to be tomorrow. I have done a lot of things in my life that I am not proud of, but after all that, *God still loves me!* He is using me to let others know it doesn't matter what you have done in the past. He will always be there no matter what."

Each individual who experiences a new beginning through CareerLink and Holistic Hardware impacts another life. It's God's domino effect!

## HERE WE GO AGAIN!

Remember Joe, who was helped by Patrick, who was helped by Mark?

Patrick threw a graduation party for Joe and made it an evangelistic event. Close to 80 people showed up for lunch and heard the story of Joe's transformed life.

Danny was one of the 80. After Danny had heard about Joe's success, Mark asked Danny if he had ever experienced God's life-changing power. "I've been waiting my whole life for someone to tell me about this!" Danny replied. Mark shared the Gospel with him, and Danny prayed right there, asking Christ into his life.

Danny plunged right into his new life. He started taking the Holistic Hardware course and attending Bible study and prayer meetings at The Lamb's. Soon, Danny landed a full-time job. I would tell you how the story ends, but it never does!...

# IMPACT SPOTLIGHT

## HOLISTIC HARDWARE LEADER ARMS INMATES WITH PRACTICAL LIFE HELP

At the jail in Cherokee County, Georgia, Holistic Hardware leader Ithiel, a part of the HLIC Prison Ministry staff, has incorporated this program's concepts ... and very effectively.

Ithiel was already well known there for his weekly church service. When he spread the word among nearly 500 inmates that he would be offering a course helping with life skills, demand was great.

The facility houses mostly inmates who are awaiting trial or have been sentenced by the courts and are awaiting transfer in the state penal system, so there is a lot of transience. To reach everyone means offering the course repeatedly. Ithiel offers the course every week, on three different days. There are more than 20 inmates in each group. Close to 200 men have gone through the 10-week course in the past year. Because of such high demand, Ithiel has even trained some Holistic Hardware graduates to lead sessions.

"These guys are looking for God's help," Ithiel says. "I see them actively putting the principles into their lives!"

# HERE'S LIFE
# PRISON MINISTRY

The Prison Ministry of Here's Life Inner City has a two-fold emphasis:

A focus on incarcerated prisoners.

Training for inner-city churches. We offer local ministries a special training manual called *Beyond Bars* to show them how to care for the families of those who are currently incarcerated and how to disciple ex-offenders released from prison or jail.

---

There are four steps in the Holistic Hardware "Responsibility Tool": Step Back, Look Back, Get Out, and Take Note.

"If Step Back, Look Back, Get Out, and Take Note does not mean anything to you, you are unprepared. During my stay here, this principle has not only helped me with life crisis but everyday encounters as well. The brothers here have made it a very popular saying. Jesus told the disciples to be ready. Thanks to Holistic Hardware, I, like David, have my stones (tools) to defeat my giant of crack addiction. The classes have been a great source of motivation and an inspiration to many of the brothers here. We are not just concerned with getting out but staying out. Now we have something we can apply and get results to live a productive life."

**—Tim, an inmate**
**(After his graduation from Holistic Hardware, Tim learned to lead sessions on his own.)**

"The Holistic Hardware toolkit has proved to be a valuable tool for helping me overcome one of the most critical personal crises I faced when I came into the Detention Center. Aspects of this personal crisis were my low self-esteem and lack of personal responsibility. I use the Responsibility Tool — the four steps — to assess my life situation daily. The Holistic Hardware tools I have learned to use have contributed tremendously toward building my personal faith in God. These Holistic Hardware skills have allowed me to more readily apply and use God's Word, the Holy Bible, to guide my life to become a true steward for Him to use. I see the fruits of His Holy Spirit growing abundantly in my life, and these skills are clearly helping me to become the man God wants me to become in Christ Jesus."

**—Anthony, an inmate**

# VICTORY IN ATLANTA!

Victory Outreach Atlanta is a powerful local ministry founded by a former heroin addict who wanted to bring the Gospel to the neediest in the inner city of Atlanta. They use Holistic Hardware, our biblically-based 10-video life skills course, as part of their program to empower drug addicts, ex-offenders, juveniles, and others.

One member of the Victory Outreach church lived next door to a crack house. The neighbor took a flier about the Holistic Hardware program next door and urged everyone he saw at the house to attend ... including Mitch.

Mitch frequented the crack house and his life was spinning out of control. He decided that it couldn't hurt to try the program. It changed his life — Mitch committed his life to Christ! He began to grow and put the principles of Holistic Hardware to use in his life. Now Mitch is free of drugs and a trusted leader at Victory Outreach.

Mitch later learned that volunteers at the church been praying specifically for all who entered the crack house!

# Chapter 7

# TOO FAR
# GONE?

*"For just as the Father raises the dead
and gives them life, even so the Son
gives life to whom
he is pleased to give it."*

JOHN 5:21

The disciples probably thought Jesus had lost His mind.

Here they were, standing in front of a cave where a dead man lay. A curious crowd was gathering, and Jesus had just given an order to remove the entrance stone!

Even the grieving sister thought it was a bad idea: "'But, Lord,' said Martha, the sister of the dead man, 'by this time there is a bad odor, for he has been there *four days*'" (John 11:39).

Four days! What was He thinking? The man was too far gone to help. He was just a corpse.

This was not only a waste of time, but bad publicity. Oh, no....

*"Lazarus, come forth!"*

Great. They were all there to help people, of course, and good intentions are one thing. But this was going too far.

*What was that?* The disciples looked at each other, then at Jesus, and then quickly back to the cave. For one long moment, no one said a word ... no one even breathed. All eyes were trained on the opening of that tomb.

"The dead man came out, his hands and feet wrapped with strips of linen, and a cloth around his face. Jesus said to them, 'Take off the grave clothes and let him go'" (John 11:44).

Once they had picked their chins up off the ground, the disciples and all who stood at the cave that day should have realized an important principle —

*No one is too far gone for the lifesaving power of God Almighty.*

Sadly, I am reminded of Lazarus when I consider the needy people of urban America. Too many are like walking dead — they have been robbed of life's hope. These men, women, and children are suffering heavy blows from poverty, drug and alcohol addiction, physical abuse, and more. Worst of all, many have not found life in Christ ... they are spiritually dead.

Here's Life Inner City workers and volunteers sometimes feel helpless to restore life and hope to many of those who are hurting. You can't blame them. The task seems impossible in some cases. Workers at the S.A.Y Yes! Center of Crossroads of the Rockies church in Denver, Colorado, certainly felt that way the first time they saw 5-year-old Rhiannon.

Her dad was violently swearing at her and dragging her tiny frail body along the sidewalk. The sight broke their hearts, and the entire staff made her a prayer project.

They had no idea what her name was, where she lived, or how to reach her. So they prayed ... and prayed ... and prayed. Months went by. A year passed. Was her situation too far gone?

Then one day, without warning, her father showed up at the Center — to register Rhiannon for summer camp!

The staff was overjoyed by the chance to impact this little girl, but they were soon taken aback as they began to discover horrible facts about Rhiannon's tragic life.

Both parents were heavy drinkers. Her mother was not only seriously depressed but also terrified to leave her home. The family lived in a backyard shed with no electricity, no running water, and no heat. The landlord occasionally let them in his house to use the bathroom or take a bath. Neither parent had a job.

It was no surprise when the staff found out that this little girl was fascinated by violent, morbid things. She flinched and twitched constantly. But after settling in to the camp, Rhiannon gradually began to relax. At one point she actually laughed, and then she began to give hugs! To top it all off, Rhiannon received a brand-new pair of shoes for fall. She beamed as she held up the box containing the new shoes, just her size.

The shoes were the link, and Rhiannon started attending church. Her parents came, too, and eventually committed their hearts to the Lord. They still struggle, but Rhiannon's father has stayed clean, and today he is holding down a regular job.

The HLIC fall shoe distribution program is called Heart & Sole. Through the generosity of our ministry friends, we send new shoes to churches and missions for distribution to needy children before school starts.

This family found new life because of unrelenting prayers and compassionate care ... expressed through something as simple as a new pair of shoes!

> Last year, we provided 2,000 brand-new school shoes to children.

## GANG TERRITORY

If ever a breath of life was needed, it was in the Brooklyn neighborhood surrounding the Spanish-speaking church of Iglesia La Hermosa.

The entire area was caught in the death grip of the Latino gang Nieta. The gang targeted pre-teen and early teen boys. Even those who were not actively involved in the gang began to model their speaking and dress after gang members. You could almost smell the stench of spiritual death in the neighborhood.

The church's pastor decided to fight the disease of gangs by launching Royal Rangers — a program that helps boys ages 5 to 17 learn about God and develop strength of character and good habits.

Two brothers, 12-year-old Carlos and 15-year-old Rudy, came to Royal Rangers with some friends. But they were troublemakers with a capital "T."

The pair would not pay attention; they distracted others. They seemed beyond help — and they were dragging the entire group down. Program director Hector was at the end of his rope with these two.

One day, he asked the boys to help him unload some resources that the church had received from Here's Life Inner City. As they were working, they came across leather sneakers — and their faces lit up!

They really wanted — and needed — those sneakers.

Their father had lost his job and couldn't support the family. They were about to lose their home. The boys' clothes were always worn and their shoes had holes in them. The tattered shoes made them a particular target for ridicule at school.

> These are quality shoes obtained at a substantial discount from manufacturers. They're not expensive, high-end shoes, nor are they hand-me-downs. These will pass the "cool test" with any kid at any school!

So Hector made a deal with the troubled brothers. He told them if they would cooperate and pay attention during Royal Rangers, he would give them the shoes.

That was just the motivation that Carlos and Rudy needed! They listened, participated, and worked hard at projects. Hector soon gave them the shoes.

Carlos and Rudy continued to grow. They began attending church and listened with respect. Today, they call Hector "hermano" — brother — and show him their greatly improved report cards from school. They also help out around the church with things like volunteering to pack Easter Bags.

These brothers went from "too far gone" to "on-the-go" for Christ — in their brand-new sneakers!

*Chapter 8*

# WHO? WHAT? WHEN? WHERE? WHY? HOW?

*"For I know the plans I have for you,'*
*declares the Lord, 'plans to prosper you*
*and not to harm you,*
*plans to give you hope*
*and a future.'"*

JEREMIAH 29:11

There were a lot of things 6-year-old Michael didn't understand.

He didn't understand why he and his father stopped living with his mom and four step-siblings.

Michael didn't know why they began going to church for the first time in his life. And he had no idea what his dad was talking about when he said he was "saved." Saved from what?

But there was one thing Michael was perfectly clear on — *how to have fun*.

And he found plenty of that at his new church's S.A.Y. Yes! Center in Louisville, Kentucky — *especially when college students came for the summer* to play with him, read him Bible stories, take him on field trips, and help him on cool arts and crafts projects.

It was one of these Summer in the City volunteers who changed Michael's life.

One day they were making bead bracelets, and as they worked, the college student explained to Michael what each bead's color represented:

- Yellow for the light of God's love …

- Blue for the sadness that sin causes …

- Red for the blood of Jesus, shed for our salvation …

- Clear — or "see-through" — for the cleansing of our sins …

- Finally, green — for growing in Christ!

It was a simple message, but powerful ... and it made sense to Michael. In fact, this very basic explanation of salvation opened his eyes and heart. Right then and there, Michael asked Jesus to come into his heart.

> College students who participate in Summer in the City volunteer for the sweat, tears, prayers, and hard work, day after day.

Now Michael not only knows what "saved" means ... he *is* saved!

Michael and thousands of other children and adults are impacted each year by a special group of volunteers participating in a unique Here's Life Inner City program —

## WHO? WHAT?

Every year, college students reach out to the urban poor during our annual Summer in the City campaign. The students come from all over — even overseas — to make an eternal difference for children like Michael. Distributing bracelets is not the only way these volunteers help share the love of Christ through inner-city churches and missions.

## WHEN?

In one of the most effective evangelistic traditions of our Campus Crusade ministry, students commit *four or eight weeks of their summer vacation* to serve in the inner city.

## WHERE?

Students work in teams of four to five on projects in cities like New York, Seattle, Los Angeles, Chicago, Denver, Louisville, Detroit, Atlanta, and Minneapolis/St. Paul.

## WHY?

Most have never been among the poor in an inner city before, but they feel strongly called by God to impact lives ... and share the clear truth of Christ.

## HOW?

They assist inner-city churches and ministries. They work in day camps, soup kitchens, rehab centers, mentoring programs, and Bible clubs.

One student volunteer, Jen, wasn't quite sure how clear her message was to Maria, a woman she found sitting on a park bench. Because Maria's first language was Spanish, Jen couldn't tell if she understood her words about the love of God ... until she saw tears forming in the woman's eyes.

> Student volunteers help with day camps and evangelistic outreaches ... provide food and hope through rescue missions ... minister to drug addicts, battered women, and AIDS victims ... lead Bible clubs for local youngsters ... and more.

After Maria prayed and asked Christ into her life, she told Jen how obvious it was to her that God had arranged their meeting. She was not from the neighborhood; she had just come on an errand. Because of recent surgery, the shopping tired her out, so she sought out the park for a brief rest. Later that week, she and her family were *moving to Puerto Rico*! But in this narrow window of opportunity, God brought Jen to her, to reveal His Word to her!

God uses these students to connect with people like Michael and Maria who need answers about God's love. But the inner-city poor are not the only ones who gain understanding. The students themselves find it a life-changing experience.

For Tiffany, Summer in the City was a turning point. She had decided early in life to become a doctor and pursued that vision wholeheartedly. She wanted to live in the suburbs, have two kids, and drive a minivan. The last thing she wanted was to end up in the inner city.

But as a sophomore at Ohio State, Tiffany went to Chicago for a week of Here's Life Inner City's Urban Immersion program — a spring break version of Summer in the City. She followed up with Summer in the City there the next season. And God began to change her heart.

Tiffany met people who broke down stereotypes. She studied Scripture and realized that Jesus offered both physical and spiritual food. He had a heart of compassion for people in need, and He began to develop that in her.

Because Tiffany is fluent in Spanish, one of the sites she served during Summer in the City was La Villita, where she worked with a summer day camp. After Tiffany returned to college, she received a letter from the director of youth at La Villita challenging her to return. Tiffany did return to Chicago after graduation, first doing campus ministry but eventually focusing on the inner city.

She began to work for La Villita, and soon found herself in the position of director of their S.A.Y. Yes! Center.

Summer in the City helped Tiffany understand that God's plan for her life was much more exciting and fulfilling than her own!

"'For I know the plans I have for you,' declares the Lord, 'plans to prosper you and not to harm you, plans to give you hope and a future.'" (Jeremiah 29:11).

This is the same message we share with those who have become hopeless and disillusioned.

> "On my last day at the Center, I had the opportunity to share Christ with a boy named Michael. I was so excited because I've never really had the opportunity to share with children. I had always felt inadequate and uneasy when approaching people with the Gospel because I was afraid of their reactions toward me. I never had allowed God to fully empower or direct me with His Holy Spirit until that day I shared with Michael. Michael eagerly prayed and received Christ as his Savior, and is now a precious child of God! I praise God that Michael is now my little brother in Christ. Seeing the Holy Spirit speak through me was one of the most exciting moments in my life."
>
> **— Purdue University student who volunteered in Louisville, Kentucky**

The urban poor have many questions: Who loves me? Why am I in this situation? What can you do to help me? How will I survive tomorrow? When will my life get better? Where is God?

Joy-filled college students, caring supporters like you, and loving local volunteers are giving them answers, with acts of love and kindness, through the unique outreaches of Here's Life Inner City.

# "WHO CARES ABOUT ME?"

Ohio University student Diane met Eddie, a homeless man, while in New York City for Urban Immersion over spring break. She was ministering at Coney Island when she saw him. They talked for a while, and she shared Christ with him. He wasn't ready to receive Christ, so Diane promised she would pray for him. When she went back to Ohio, that's what she did; she prayed for him daily.

When she came back for Summer in the City, Diane's first ministry site was Salt & Sea at Coney Island. She asked the director about Eddie. But Eddie hadn't been seen in three months.

Still Diane prayed, and during her first day in the neighborhood, she spotted him near the subway. Again she talked with him about Christ and how much God loved him. When he realized that Diane had been praying for him for months, Eddie began to cry. He realized how much God loved him — and he asked Christ into his life.

Today, Eddie is connected with the Salt & Sea Mission for help and encouragement. God cares!

# AT THE CORNER LIQUOR STORE — THE PERFECT PLACE TO MEET JESUS

Tabernacle Missionary Baptist Church in Detroit sent an evangelism team with a group of Summer in the City students to knock on doors. One group that had been assigned to a particular block found out there weren't many homes there, so moved on to the next block. They found themselves on the corner in front of a liquor store ... which also served as the neighborhood crack station. Many people were lingering on the sidewalk outside, so the team went to work.

One man began to cry as soon as they approached him. As they talked about Jesus, he said, "I really need to know Jesus. I need to be saved!" He prayed on the spot.

A woman waiting at a nearby bus stop watched the prayers and conversations in front of the liquor store. Buses came and went. Finally, she walked over and admitted that she had received Christ as a child, but had been away from Him for a long time. "Tell me how I can come back," she pleaded.

Some of the students even went in to talk to the owner of the liquor store (who was also the crack dealer). In all, four people received Christ and one recommitted her life to Christ. Members of the church are following up on all the new converts.

# *Chapter 9*

# A GIFT ...

# JUST

# FOR YOU

*"But the gift of God
is eternal life in
Christ Jesus
our Lord."*

ROMANS 6:23

Every Easter, volunteers from inner-city churches and outreaches across America arm themselves with some of the most powerful evangelistic tools to date — Here's Life Easter Bags — and fan out into the poorest neighborhoods to share the Good News of Jesus Christ.

What's the point, you ask? What does a gift of candy and trinkets have to do with the Resurrection of our Lord and Savior? Hmmm.

Let me explain by sharing with you one of my favorite Easter stories.

For three years, Cassandra led a weekly Bible study in Jacksonville, Florida, for women living in a halfway house after release from prison.

Of the 28 residents, only 12 attended the Bible study.

> Our Easter Bags are filled with things inner-city children treasure: candy, fruit, crayons, a toy — plus a Bible activity book designed for children with little church background.

The rest avoided Cassandra at all costs. When she came around, they headed upstairs (where visitors were not allowed) and stayed until she left. Cassandra prayed and prayed about it, but she never could connect with them. They just didn't want to talk to her.

Shortly before Easter, Cassandra decided to bring a box of Here's Life Easter Bags for the children who visited their mothers in the shelter.

These bags — filled with candy, fruit, crayons, a toy, plus a Bible activity book — are always a big hit with inner-city kids. But Cassandra had no idea the impact they would make on the adults.

When she reached into the box, pulled out some Easter Bags, and said they were gifts for the women's children, all the residents began to come toward her.

Cassandra began talking with them, giving them Easter Bags. The children who were there happily grabbed bags and began digging through the contents.

## CELINDA'S DECISION

In the midst of all this, one woman named Celinda walked right up to Cassandra. At first Cassandra felt a little apprehensive — this was one tough-looking lady. But Celinda said, "I need to give my life to Christ. I've been messing around, not doing right. I need to turn my life around."

Cassandra shared the Gospel with Celinda, and she responded, promising to attend the Bible study. But the next week she wasn't there. Five weeks went by before Celinda actually showed up at the study. The first time she attended, she cried most of the time. Afterward, she confessed that she had been sitting at the top of the stairs listening each week, but she felt too ashamed to actually walk in.

Celinda admitted that she had received Christ as a child but had turned away, getting in with the wrong crowd and doing some bad things that landed her in prison. She had a baby while in prison — her little boy was now nine months old. She knew she needed to come back to the Lord. The talk with Cassandra — set in motion by the Easter Bags — was her turning point.

Inner-city churches, missions, and ministries distribute more than 30,000 Easter Bags each year to connect with children in their neighborhoods ... sharing the Gospel and building long-term relationships with their families.

The Easter Bag distribution began a change in Cassandra's relationship with the other women of the shelter, too. Today, instead of avoiding her, they wave and say hello when she comes in!

It seems impossible that something as simple as an Easter Bag can make such a difference ... but we see it happen over and over. The contents of the Bags themselves — simple joys used to celebrate Easter — aren't as powerful as the act of love demonstrated in the giving of them.

This, after all, is what Christ's resurrection was ... a gift of love to each of us, delivered on Easter. We are recipients of the most incredible gift in the history of mankind — salvation.

For Celinda and the other women of the halfway house and their children, a simple gift of candy and toys was a symbol of God's love in action ... an introduction to the gift God gave on that first Easter 2,000 years ago.

# TESTIMONY SPOTLIGHT

## MEET WILLIAM....

William, at age 12, is the oldest of three children who live in a welfare motel in Bell Gardens, near downtown Los Angeles, with their mother. While his mom works, William is responsible for his younger siblings.

Southland Church is located nearby. Every Saturday, the church has a program called "Jesus and Me," or "JAM," for children from the church and the neighborhood.

Volunteers noticed William's captivating smile and gentleness, qualities rarely found in the "motel kids." He attended JAM off and on, but unfortunately missed more than he came. His mother was usually gone on Saturday mornings, and he had to stay with his siblings.

On the Saturday before Easter, the church had a special "Jesus and Me" Children's Church featuring Easter Bags provided by Here's Life Inner City. The bus filled to capacity with boys and girls eager to come and receive their Bags. William was in the crowd.

The service featured singing, games, and a special video depicting the Easter story.

At the end of the service, many children, including William, came forward to receive the risen Savior. One of the workers gave William a Bible. "I love Jesus," William told a JAM organizer a few weeks later, "and Jesus loves me." He had been reading his Bible and praying, he also reported — and doing his homework, too!

A 12-year-old boy living in a drug-infested motel may not have much of a chance for a good life. But that's just the natural odds. With Jesus, William has supernatural chances ... true hope for a future.

# SO GOD, WHAT'S ON *YOUR* MIND?

Rather than ask "*what* is on God's mind?" maybe the question should be "*who?*" I believe at the top of that list are names like Rhiannon, Michael, Jenny, Carlos, Kesha, William, and thousands upon thousands of others just like them.

The poor and needy are on God's mind. They're in His heart.

"The poor and needy search for water, but there is none; their tongues are parched with thirst," God says in Isaiah 41:17. "But I the Lord will answer them; I, the God of Israel, will not forsake them."

God's compassion for the poor runs deep. In the Old Testament, He rebuked His people for neglecting the needy. When Jesus was born, it was into poverty. In Luke 4, Christ was very clear on His mission:

"'The Spirit of the Lord is on me, because He has anointed me to preach the good news to the poor. He has sent me to proclaim freedom for the prisoners and recovery of sight for the blind, to release the oppressed, to proclaim the year of the Lord's favor'" (Luke 4:18-19).

God repeatedly calls us to love and care for the poor. Paul, James, John, and Peter did as well. "Suppose a brother or sister is without clothes and daily food," James observed. "If one of you says to him, 'Go, I wish you well; keep warm and well fed,' but does nothing about his physical needs, what good is it? In the same way, faith by itself, if it is not accompanied by action, is dead" (James 2:15-17).

Scripture states that whoever cares for the needy honors God, and He promises to bless those who help the poor. "And if anyone gives even a cup of cold water to one of these little ones because he is my disciple, I tell you the truth, he will certainly not lose his reward" (Matthew 10:42).

Certainly, there are greater concentrations of the poor in our cities than anywhere else. The Bible records Jesus weeping only twice, once was for a lost city — Jerusalem. Cities are referenced over 1,250 times in the Bible.

God's twin concerns — for the poor and for the cities — come together in the ministry of Here's Life Inner City. God's heart for the urban poor is reflected in our mission philosophy: to serve and mobilize the Church to live out God's heart for the poor and fulfill the Great Commission.

When Peter, James, and John gave Paul the right hand of fellowship and sent him on his missionary journey, Paul said, "All they asked was that we should remember the poor, the very thing I was eager to do."

In this same way, as you have met the people touched by Here's Life in the pages of this book, I pray that you will join us in experiencing this great privilege ... to emulate Christ in the cities. By your love and God's grace, lives will be reached for eternity.

What an incredible impact we can make as Christ's arms extended ....

# MAKING A DIFFERENCE

Martin and his friend Eric are both Washington, D.C., businessmen. They meet regularly for fellowship and to encourage each other in their walk with God. They often talk about what it means to love God with all your heart, soul, mind, and strength and to love your neighbor as yourself.

Martin and Eric studied the parable of the Good Samaritan, too, and passages in 1 John. Their conclusion: If we don't find ways to love others — especially others who are different from us — we have to question our love for God.

On that basis, they determined to do something — they just didn't know what.

After Martin and Eric had lunch together one day, they walked past two homeless men who asked them for help. The friends passed on by without a thought — but by the time they reached the next block they were struck by what had happened. They'd been seeking a way to express love ... and here was their opportunity!

They bought some food and took it back to the men. Then they sat and talked with them as they ate. They uncovered needs and offered prayer, and the needy men were warmly receptive. One came to Martin's church that Sunday, and later that week, Martin took him to visit a residential program at a downtown mission.

God was beginning to develop in Martin a deep concern for the poor. He enlisted others from his church, and they began to provide food for the needy as they encountered them.

That winter in Washington was colder than usual. Martin learned about Here's Life Homeless Care Kits and arranged to receive 25 on behalf of his downtown D.C. church. He and the other volunteers went out on a very cold day looking for people they could bless with the Kits.

The first two men Martin and his group met were very responsive. They eagerly received the blankets and other warm items, and they listened to the Gospel message. Both prayed, asking Jesus to forgive them and come into their lives.

The next Sunday, the men showed up at Martin's church. It was the start of a special relationship between Martin and one of the men, named John. John suffers from depression and has difficulty holding a job. But he meets regularly with Martin to talk about faith. And John eagerly reads material Martin gives him. He's had trouble believing that the power of the Gospel is enough to change him, but Martin is encouraging him to keep at it, and to get involved with a supportive group of believers who can support him.

Martin and his friends are learning a lot through their contact with the poor. They see God at work as they trust Him outside of their "comfort zone." And they realize, now more strongly than ever, that to whom much is given, much is expected.

As they persevere, they are making a real difference ... one heart at a time.

This is our mission, our mandate.

Today's Church must reach out with practical love and tangible compassion to the poor. Here are some ways you can fulfill God's call to you to reach the needy through Here's Life Inner City:

## PRAY

Prayer is a spiritual tool that crosses all geographical and cultural boundaries. It is a direct line of communication to God that you can use to impact others. You can ask God daily to use Here's Life to reach the poor and needy across the United States by praying for:

> ... the people of specific cities that we reach into with our partnerships.

> ... those impacted by specific programs.

> ... the many volunteers and workers of Here's Life, and the local churches and missions who use our resources to touch their communities.

> ... the ever-expanding reach of Here's Life as God leads.

> ... individuals who are hurting. You don't have to know their names — God does.

I encourage you to pray with your family, and in your Sunday school class or Bible study group. Get your friends, your family, and your church to be part of our ministry through prayer.

"Finally, brothers, pray for us that the message of the Lord may spread rapidly and be honored, just as it was with you" (2 Thessalonians 3:1).

## VOLUNTEER

If your church or community has a partnership with Here's Life Inner City to distribute food, shoes, or Easter Bags, get involved. Volunteer to sort goods, deliver products, or just answer the phones. God will bless every effort. Maybe your church or community has its own program. Find out what you can do. We are all striving for the same goal — to share Christ's love and hope in a practical way to the hurting people of our inner cities.

If the Lord has called you to reach out in ministry to the inner-city poor, we may be able to help. College students may want to investigate Summer in the City or Urban Immersion (spring break) for short-term mission opportunities. Churches may want to initiate a S.A.Y. Yes! Center for Youth Development or develop a life-skills course using our Holistic Hardware resources. If you want to know more about our partnerships with community churches and missions, call us at 212.494.0321, check out our website at www.hlic.org, or write us at Here's Life Inner City, 142 West 36th Street, New York, NY 10018.

## GIVE

Here's Life Inner City could do nothing without the financial support of caring Christians. We are the urban ministry of Campus Crusade for Christ. As such, we are a non-profit organization and rely on the gifts of churches and individuals like you. Your giving empowers us to help people like Maria, Spring, Vivian, and Tommy. We are able to go out to the homeless, the hungry, and the hurting because of your faithfulness to answer God's commission to reach the poor.

Your gift today will help us continue feeding hungry families in Christ's name. You can help us open more S.A.Y. Yes! Centers, distribute more Boxes of Love, shoes, Easter Bags, Homeless Care Kits, and so much more. You will be giving education and resources to help the hopeless find jobs.

Please use one of the enclosed reply pages to support the many outreaches of Here's Life Inner City as God leads.

Your generosity will help us be there — offering real help for real people in desperate need. Your action today will help us write tomorrow's stories of lives impacted by the love and compassion of Jesus Christ. Thank you.

*"For I was hungry and you gave me something to eat, I was thirsty and you gave me something to drink, I was a stranger and you invited me in,*

*"I needed clothes and you clothed me, I was sick and you looked after me, I was in prison and you came to visit me.'*

*"Then the righteous will answer him, 'Lord, when did we see you hungry and feed you, or thirsty and give you something to drink?*

*'When did we see you a stranger and invite you in, or needing clothes and clothe you?*

*'When did we see you sick or in prison and go to visit you?'*

*"The King will reply, 'I tell you the truth, whatever you did for one of the least of these brothers of mine, you did for me.'"*

MATTHEW 25:35-40

# SHARING CHRIST THROUGH **BOXES OF LOVE**!

❏ **Yes, Ted!** I want to help meet the physical and spiritual needs of hungry inner-city families for Thanksgiving by providing complete holiday dinners through the Boxes of Love outreach, while continuing the compassionate evangelistic outreaches to the urban poor through Here's Life Inner City. Enclosed is my gift of:

### PRACTICAL COMPASSION

One of our partner ministries in Queens, New York, delivered a Box of Love to a grandmother who was struggling to raise seven grandchildren, ages 2 to 13.

The children's parents were both addicted to drugs — and Grandma Miriam felt hopeless.

When one of the local church's volunteers took a Box of Love (filled with turkey and the trimmings, bread, yams, vegetables, dessert, Scripture verses, and a children's book) to Miriam's home, she and the children were thrilled to see so much food! Now they attend church faithfully.

Jesus has made the difference in their lives!

❏ $73.42 to feed 2 families of up to 6

❏ $36.71 to feed 1 family of up to 6

❏ $110.13 to feed 3 families of up to 6

❏ $146.84 to feed 4 families of up to 6

❏ $500

❏ $1,000

❏ $_____ to feed as many families as possible

*[To give by credit card, please see reverse side]*

---

NAME

---

ADDRESS

---

ADDRESS

---

CITY, STATE, ZIP

**2289571  TT1200**

*Thank you for your love and generosity! Please make your tax-deductible check payable to Here's Life Inner City and return to: Here's Life Inner City · 142 West 36th Street · New York, NY 10018. Here's Life Inner City is the compassionate urban ministry of Campus Crusade for Christ.*

## For credit card donations:

❑ VISA    ❑ MasterCard    ❑ American Express

❑ Discover    ❑ Diner's Club

_____
CREDIT CARD #

_____
EXPIRATION DATE

_____
SIGNATURE

# SENDING HOPE TO THE **HOMELESS**

❏ **Yes, Ted!** I'll stand with Here's Life Inner City to share the Gospel and the love of Christ through the contents of Homeless Care Kits for homeless children or adults during the bitter winter months and extend all our ministries together. Enclosed is my gift of hope of:

❏ $66 to reach 2 homeless children or adults

❏ $33 to reach 1 ❏ $99 to reach 3

❏ $132 to reach 4 ❏ $330 to reach 10

❏ $_____ to help as many as possible

*[To give by credit card, please see reverse side]*

## LOVE IN ACTION

Monica is a 32-year-old Chicago native who is HIV-positive and who has battled drug addiction for years. Because of her dangerous lifestyle, the state of Illinois gave custody of her five children to Monica's mother.

Last year, during Chicago's cold, deadly winter, Monica was living on the streets. She took shelter in abandoned buildings when she could find them — but she couldn't escape the bitter cold. When Monica heard that Galilee Baptist Church was handing out Homeless Care Kits filled with a blanket, hat, gloves, and toiletries, she showed up — eager for a blanket. But what Monica received was so much more.

The people at the church welcomed her and prayed for her. They encouraged her to turn her life over to God — and invited her to church. Monica showed up that Sunday — and the next. And it wasn't long before she opened her heart to Christ.

Quick to admit that she's a "work in progress," Monica nonetheless attends church regularly. Monica now lives with her children at her mother's home.

_____
NAME

_____
ADDRESS

_____
ADDRESS

_____
CITY, STATE, ZIP

**2290723 TT1205**

*Thank you for your love and generosity! Please make your tax-deductible check payable to Here's Life Inner City and return to: Here's Life Inner City · 142 West 36th Street · New York, NY 10018. Here's Life Inner City is the compassionate urban ministry of Campus Crusade for Christ.*

## For credit card donations:

❑ VISA          ❑ MasterCard          ❑ American Express

❑ Discover      ❑ Diner's Club

_____

CREDIT CARD #

_____

EXPIRATION DATE

_____

SIGNATURE

# HERE'S LIFE
# INNER CITY
# WAREHOUSES

## Distributing God's resources, feeding His children

❏ **Yes, Ted!** I want to help give the hungry in urban America food and necessities through the distribution from the Here's Life regional warehouses. Please use my gift to further the ministry of the warehouses and continue all the outreaches of Here's Life. I have enclosed a gift of:

❏ $30 to help provide 60 meals
❏ $50 to help provide 100 meals
❏ $100 to help provide 200 meals
❏ $_____ to help as many as possible

*[To give by credit card, please see reverse side]*

God is using five regional warehouses — in New York, Los Angeles, Chicago, Minneapolis, and Bakersfield — to provide food for more than 450,000 people each month: the single mom struggling to feed her children ... the elderly couple with no family and no one who cares ... the family devastated by layoffs.

Through the giving and generosity of friends like you, we provide food, baby items, clothing, and more for distribution by local churches and missions. But there are so many more needy people waiting on help. Your gift today could mean the difference between supper and going to bed hungry for quite a few children.

Please give as God leads, and He will reward your sacrifice. "'And if anyone gives even a cup of cold water to one of these little ones because he is my disciple, I tell you the truth, he will certainly not lose his reward'" (Matthew 10:42).

_____
NAME

_____
ADDRESS

_____
ADDRESS

_____
CITY, STATE, ZIP                    **2290926 TT1210**

*Thank you for your love and generosity! Please make your tax-deductible check payable to Here's Life Inner City and return to: Here's Life Inner City · 142 West 36th Street · New York, NY 10018. Here's Life Inner City is the compassionate urban ministry of Campus Crusade for Christ.*

# For credit card donations:

❏ VISA            ❏ MasterCard            ❏ American Express

❏ Discover        ❏ Diner's Club

_____
CREDIT CARD #

_____
EXPIRATION DATE

_____
SIGNATURE

# COMPASSION BY COMMAND

HERE'S LIFE INNER CITY HAS PUT THE LESSONS OF
20+ YEARS OF MINISTRY TO THE URBAN POOR INTO
AN INNOVATIVE RESOURCE FOR YOUR CHURCH.

**GREAT FOR BIBLE STUDY GROUPS ...
SUNDAY SCHOOL CLASSES ...
A CHURCH SERIES!**

Scripture commands the Church to have compassion for the poor. It is both
a responsibility and a privilege.

*"He who oppresses the poor shows contempt for their Maker, but whoever
is kind to the needy honors God"* (Proverbs 14:31).

Here's Life Inner City has designed a 7-week video and Bible study package
with teacher and student study guides to help your church explore the
issues of poverty and discover biblical directives related to the poor.

## You will be touched by real life stories.

## Your church will find practical steps to help you make a difference in your community.

FEATURING THE MADE-FOR-TV MOVIE,
**GOD BLESS THE CHILD,**
STARRING ACADEMY AWARD NOMINEE
**MARE WINNINGHAM**.

Understand God's heart for the poor and how it impacts you and your
church today! Compassion by Command will give you the answers you need
to impact your world ... one hurting person at a time.

GO TO **www.compassionbycommand.com**
OR CALL **800-827-2788** TO ORDER YOUR
COMPLETE COMPASSION BY COMMAND KIT!
**COST: $50 DVD, $75 VHS**

# MINISTRY
# OPPORTUNITIES
# THROUGH HLIC

HLIC is the compassionate urban ministry of Campus Crusade for Christ International. Our mission is to "mobilize and serve the church to live out God's heart for the poor and fulfill the Great Commission."

This is accomplished through 170 "urban missionaries" and thousands of volunteers on 18 city teams who empower churches and missions to help their less fortunate neighbors. Resource areas include food and clothing distribution, after-school programs, life skills training, spiritual help, and so much more.

Teams currently operate in the following cities:

| | | |
|---|---|---|
| Atlanta | Detroit | Minneapolis/St. Paul |
| Bakersfield | Jacksonville | New York |
| Central Arkansas | Kansas City | Orlando |
| Chicago | Los Angeles | Philadelphia |
| Colorado Springs | Louisville | Seattle |
| Denver | Milwaukee | Washington, D.C. |

If you would like information about volunteering in one of these cities or joining our staff, check the HLIC website www.hlic.org or contact our National HLIC Office:

142 West 36 Street, New York, NY 10044   212.494.0321

# WANT TO GO
# FURTHER?

Some resources to consider!

\* Lupton, Robert. _Theirs Is the Kingdom: Celebrating the Gospel in Urban America_. San Francisco: Harper & Row, 1989. Short stories draw you warmly into Lupton's world as a pastor and minister to the poor in Atlanta. Readers are confronted with true-to-life principles of caring for people in poverty.

Perkins, John. _With Justice for All_. Ventura, CA: Regal Books, 1982. Perkins, an African-American from Mississippi, describes his personal journey of injustice and how this led to the evolution of his life principles of the three Rs of urban ministry: racial reconciliation, relocation, and redistribution. This will provide good background to some of the core issues that have fueled poverty in America's cities.

\* Sherman, Amy L. _Sharing God's Heart for the Poor_. Charlottesville, VA: 2000. Wonderful short meditations on seventeen Scriptures related to God's heart for the poor and our role in expressing His Kingdom to a world in need. Co-published by Trinity Presbyterian Church — Urban Ministries (Charlottesville, VA) and Welfare Policy Center of the Hudson Institute (Indianapolis, IN).

Sider, Ron (editor). _For They Shall Be Fed_. Dallas: Word Publishing, 1997. An exhaustive listing of Scriptures and prayers pertaining to hunger, justice, and the poor, along with devotional helps from a broad selection of Christian authors. This would be a good book for further devotional reading.

\* Sjogren, Steve and Janice. _101 Ways to Help People in Need_. US: NavPress, 2002. This book presents practical and creative ways for you and your church to reach out to people with physical, emotional, and relational needs.

\* Available for purchase as a set from Here's Life Inner City. Order the **CxC Launch Kit** by calling 800.827.2788 or through the compassionbycommand.org website.

IF YOU WOULD LIKE
TO RECEIVE
MORE INFORMATION,
PLEASE WRITE:


Here's Life Inner City
142 West 36th Street
New York, NY 10018
212.494.0321

Website: www.hlic.org